THE SUPREME
AND
HIS FOUR CHILDREN

FIVE SPIRITUAL DICTIONARIES

Sri Chinmoy

THE SUPREME
AND HIS FOUR CHILDREN
FIVE SPIRITUAL DICTIONARIES

FLEET PRESS CORPORATION

New York

Fleet Press Corporation
156 Fifth Avenue
New York City 10010

Original drawing of Sri Chinmoy by Ashok

Introduction

These five dictionaries are the inspired creation of the great Spiritual Master Sri Chinmoy. Sri Chinmoy's God-ordained mission is the blossoming of the human soul in the Divine Light. In 1964 he left India for the West, where our material and intellectual concerns have all but starved the crying spiritual child within each of us. In these eight years he has worked tirelessly for his many Centres and meditation groups in the United States, Canada, the Caribbean, Europe, and the Far East. Each week he offers his inner treasure to the United Nations as he meditates for world peace with staff members of many nationalities. He has spoken at dozens of universities and answered countless questions about meditation and the inner life. His unique identification with the needs of the struggling world compels him to give himself totally in all that he does.

In these dictionaries Sri Chinmoy, on the strength of his sublime and direct realization of the highest Truth, enters into the very essence of each word and illumines it, expands it, deepens it. Sri Chinmoy has free access to the Consciousness of the Supreme, the eternal Father, and to the souls of all His children. The aspiration of the devotee and the God-lover striving to achieve their union with God; the endless earthward sacrifice of the Yogi and the Avatar and their sweetest intimacy with the Father; and finally the exalted perfection of the

Supreme Himself—all are revealed herein. Each time we read these dictionaries they offer our hearts' recognition a new truth and a new delight, a new awareness of our life's goal and of our God's utmost eagerness to receive us.

Nemi

Sri Chinmoy

Sri Chinmoy was born in Bengal, India, in 1931. When he was twelve he entered an ashram (spiritual community) where he practiced meditation and other yogic disciplines for twenty years. In his early teens Sri Chinmoy attained the highest Transcendental Consciousness, a state of being in which the entire existence of the seeker is fused into God. This state of consciousness is rarely achieved even by great Spiritual Masters after decades of effort. Not content with his own personal realization and liberation, Sri Chinmoy has dedicated his life to serving the divine in aspiring humanity. In 1964 he followed an inner command to bring the precious fruits of his meditation to the West to feed hungry seekers here. The Master has established Centres for the study of meditation and spiritual philosophy throughout North America, Europe and Asia. His home and headquarters are in New York City.

Sri Chinmoy has lectured at 100 of the world's foremost universities, including Oxford and Cambridge. He conducts weekly meditations at the United Nations and has delivered a number of lectures there as part of the Dag Hammarskjold Series. The Guru has appeared on numerous radio and television shows.

The Master has written prolifically both prose and poetry. His writings form a self-consistent whole, covering every facet of the spiritual life. His followers study his works to achieve the mental purity *and illumination which are necessary before a higher consciousness can dawn.*

Sri Chinmoy describes his path as that of love, devotion and surrender. To an advanced seeker these three words convey an infinite depth of meaning, for they embody the essence of a lifetime of aspiration. The path is the same for all, yet Sri Chinmoy guides each disciple in a unique way, according to the soul's individual needs. As the disciples see their own ignorance, suffering and imperfection transformed into divine Light, Delight and Perfection, they realize that a true Master is the manifestation of God's Highest Grace.

Contents

A DEVOTEE'S DICTIONARY

 ## ABSENCE

*God's temporary absence
from man's heart
is called
human temptation.*

 ## BODY

*Man's body needs
total transformation.
God's Body needs
complete manifestation.*

 ## CAMEL

*Human life
is an untiring camel.
Divine life
is not only a winning deer,
but a satisfied lion.*

DUTY

Duty soulfully performed,
  Divinity triumphantly revealed.
And the only duty
  is to surrender oneself
    unconditionally and constantly
to the express Will of the Supreme.

EARTH

Earth below me grows.
  Earth within me glows.
    Earth above me sows.

FEAR

Man fears
  God's glowing Infinity.
God fears
  man's brooding stupidity.

GOD

God
    invents Love.
Man
    discovers life.

HUMILITY

In man,
   humility is
      the most important necessity.
In God,
   humility is
      the most fulfilling reality.

IGNORANCE

Ignorance
   has only two real enemies:
    Man's ascending cry
      and
    God's descending Smile.

JOY

Real joy
*   is the realisation*
*   of eternal aspiration.*

KING

An outer king is he
*   who has a vast kingdom.*
An inner king is he
*   whose kingdom of light and*
*   delight is flooded*
with God's transcendental Smile
and absolute Pride.

LOVE

I love God
*   because of*
*   my necessity's command.*
God loves me
*   because of*
*   His Divinity's demand.*

 MAN

In the outer life,
*   man's forgotten expectation*
*   is God.*
In the inner life,
*   God's conscious*
*   and constant expectation*
*   is man.*

 NAME

God's real name
*   is Compassion.*
His false name
*   is Indifference.*

 ORPHAN

A child is an orphan
*   when he loses*
*   his father and mother.*
A man is an orphan
*   when he loses*
his inner joy: his Divine Mother,
and his inner peace:
*   his Divine Father.*

 PURITY

Purity is at once
the necessity and surety
of an aspiring life.

 QUESTION

There is and there can be
only one question
here on earth
and
there in heaven:
"Who is not God?"

 REALISATION

Before realisation,
man is a minor
with a major Problem.
After realisation,
man is a major
with millions of minor problems
created by his followers.

 ### SURRENDER

God is not fortunate enough
to see the earth-consciousness
surrendering unconditionally
to Him.

 ### TEACHER

A spiritual teacher is he
who
starves with man
and
dines with God.

 ### UNIVERSE

The universe is at once
God's grain of sand
and man's land
of infinite vast.

 VICTORY

Yesterday
    your victory's crown
        was possession.
Today
    your victory's crown
        is renunciation.
Tomorrow
    your victory's crown
        shall be liberation.

 WISDOM

Man's wisdom
    is God's pure pride.
    God's Wisdom
        is man's sure salvation.

 X-RAY

An x-ray machine examines
    my large body.
My aspiration examines
    my concern for humanity,
        my larger body.
My realisation examines
    my love for Divinity,
        my largest Body.

YEAR

*Each new year
    offers the same flaming question:
Who is going to win
    in the tug-of-war
        between
God, the Compassion,
    and
man, the imperfection?*

ZEAL

*In his outer life,
    man does not know
        what lasting zeal is.
In his inner life,
    man does not know
        if there is anything else
            other than constant zeal.*

A GOD-LOVER'S DICTIONARY

ASPIRATION

*Divine aspiration
endures.
Human fruition
wanes.*

BEAUTY

*Tempting beauty
is the weed.
Illumining beauty
is the crop.*

COURAGE

*The soul-courage
traced,
the body-fear
erased.*

DESTINY

An unconditionally
surrendered seeker
Is the divine architect
of his supreme destiny.

ETERNITY

Man needs
Eternity's life-breath.
Eternity needs
God's Soul-Glow.

FORCE

Man's mind-force
is a fleeting inspiration.
Man's soul-force
is his lasting realisation.

 *GOD-*
REALISATION

God-realisation
is a perfect stranger
to man-deception.

 *HUMANITY*

To choose the Real
is to fulfil the Ideal
of humanity.

 *INDIVIDUALITY*

Human individuality
is a self-torturing personality.
Divine individuality
is a self-discovering personality.

JUNGLE

Thicker than the thickest
 is the jungle of the mind.
Brighter than the brightest
 is the sky of the heart.

KEY

Alas, man wants to open
 God the Door
 without having
 Aspiration the key.

LIFE

Earth's life evolves.
 Heaven's life resolves.
 God's Life solves.

MAN

The brute in man
is his violence.
The human in man
is his fear.
The divine in man
is his heart's cry.

NOTHING

Without God-realisation
a seeker is nothing.
With God-realisation
he is God's Everything.

OATH

The preparatory oath
is to avoid the face
of ignorance.
The culminating oath
is to see only the Face
of God,
Within, without, below, above.

PERFECTION

God the Perfection lives
in His Concern for humanity.
God the perfect Perfection lives
in His Love for Divinity.
God the eternal Perfection lives
in His Meditation on Reality.

QUANTITY
QUALITY

Quantity
God's Compassion
always has.
Quality
God's Perfection
always is.

REALITY

God in man
is man's life-building Reality.
Man in God
is man's soul-elevating Reality.

 *SURRENDER*

Mutual surrender
is the flowering
of God's Soul
and the towering
of man's Goal.

 *TEMPTATION*

The tempting
and tempted seeker
is a dead weight
on God's Protection-Light.

 *UNION*

Man's union with God
makes God
Unconditionally gracious,
makes man
Supremely precious.

VOTE

At every second
I vote only for
The Transcendental Candidate,
my Supreme.

WALL

Man, the desiring
body-consciousness
is the only wall
that stands between
man's inmost cry
and
God's Mightiest Compassion.

XANTIPPE

Socrates' wife, Xantippe,
found her philosopher husband
unbearable.
A seeker's soul
finds the seeker's ignorance
not only unbearable,
but also inescapable.

YES

When God compassionately says,
*   "Yes!"*
man thinks that God is
*   singularly unwise.*
When God compassionately says,
*   "No!"*
man feels that God is
*   incredibly cruel.*

ZOO

When I want to see my Past,
*   I go to the zoo.*
When I want to see my Present,
*   I go deep within.*
When I want to see my Future,
*   I throw myself*
*   at the Feet of the Supreme.*

A YOGI'S DICTIONARY

 ASPIRANT

A Yogi
   is the supremely realised
   aspirant.

 BODY

A Yogi is not in the body.
   He is not of the body.
But he is for the body-
   for the transformation of the body
and for the perfection of the body.

 CONFINEMENT

Solitary confinement
   is not meant
   for a modern Yogi,
for God wants him
   to be a militant Yogi.

 *DEVOTION*

Your increasing devotion
to your Yogi-Guru
can easily tame
the wild vehemence of your mind.

 *EVOLUTION*

A Yogi
is the fastest evolution
of God.

 *FALSE*

A false Yogi
is God's true embarrassment.

 **GLORY**

*A Yogi's purest purity
is the height
of God's Glory.*

 **HUMANITY**

*A self-surrendered Yogi
is the only hope and promise
of a self-fulfilling humanity.*

 **INSPIRE**

*A map inspires you
to study a country.
A Yogi inspires you
to study God's universe
and God the Universe.*

JOY

A Yogi knows
that in order to retain
his supreme joy,
he has always to remain
the Supreme's supreme toy.

KING

The King of the Yogis
represents God the Protection.
The Queen of the Yoginis
represents God the Compassion.

LINK

Delight
is the connecting link
between a Yogi's highest realisation
and God's perfect Perfection.

 MAN

*The man in the Yogi
attempts.
The God in the Yogi
attains.*

 NAME

*God has secretly changed
the Yogi's name
into even-mindedness.
God has openly changed
the Yogi's name
into non-attachment.*

 OSCILLATION

*The disciples learn from their Yogi-Guru
that the oscillation of the mind
is the projection of their ignorance,
and that the dejection of the mind
is the deliberate rejection
of their inner elation.*

 PERFECT

A perfect Yogi
is God's endless contribution
to Mother-Earth.

 QUALIFIED

A qualified Yogi
warns his disciples
not to mistake
the outer complacency
for the inner
self-sufficiency.

 REINCARNATION

In any incarnation
a Yogi can have
his final reincarnation.

 SEA & SKY

A Yogi's mind
    is the waveless sea
and his heart
    is the cloudless sky.

 TORTURE

A real Yogi is he
    who has at once
transcended the pure torture
    and sure rapture
of the body-consciousness.

 UNION

To love, adore and worship
    a real Yogi
is to enjoy perfect union
    with God the Beloved.

 VICTORY

A Yogi's constant love for heaven
  is God's victory in the inner world.
A Yogi's supreme sacrifice for earth
  is God's victory in the outer world.

 WATER

Water distilled is pure
  because it contains nothing else.
A Yogi realised is pure
  because he embodies divinity
    and divinity alone.

 X-RAY

The medical science has no other choice
  than to cherish
a limited and imperfect x-ray machine.
Three cheers for the Yogic science,
  for it has discovered God,
the unlimited and perfect x-ray machine.

YOGI

A Yogi's life is the manifestation
of the father's love and wisdom,
the friend's care and concern,
the Master's guidance and protection,
and God's Illumination and Perfection.

ZONE

A Yogi can and does live
millions of miles away
from the zone
of cosmic ignorance.

AN AVATAR'S DICTIONARY

 **ASCENT**

An Avatar
*   is God's compassionate descent*
*   and man's conscious ascent.*

 **BIOGRAPHY**

God's biography,
*   abridged and condensed,*
*   is the earthly life*
*   of an Avatar.*

 *CAMEL*

An Avatar
*   is God's faithful camel.*
A Yogi
*   is God's faithful dog.*

DREAM

A budding Avatar
is God's fulfilling Dream.
A blossomed Avatar
is God's fulfilled Reality.

ESSENCE

An Avatar's pure essence
is God, the Absolute.
God's sure substance
is an Avatar
of the highest magnitude.

FAIL

When an Avatar fails,
God sails the Boat of Compassion.
Humanity sails the boat of
utter disappointment.
His disciples and followers
sail their boat in his
strongest justification.

 GOAL

An Avatar's inner Goal
    is God's eternal and
        transcendental Smile.
An Avatar's outer goal
    is man's ignorance freed,
        life-illumined and soul-fulfilled smile.

 HUMANITY'S
DIVINITY

An Avatar is not the monopoly
    of any individual.
An Avatar's soul
    is for Divinity's Humanity
and his heart is for Humanity's Divinity.

 INITIATION

The Avatar
    received initiation
        from God.
God receives
    completion
        from the Avatar.

 JOY

By serving God constantly,
an Avatar gets satisfying joy.
By helping suffering mankind,
an Avatar gets satisfied joy.

 KINGDOM

God's inner Kingdom
is an Avatar's eyes.
God's outer Kingdom
is an Avatar's voice.

 LIFE

An Avatar
is the Life of man's
secret God.

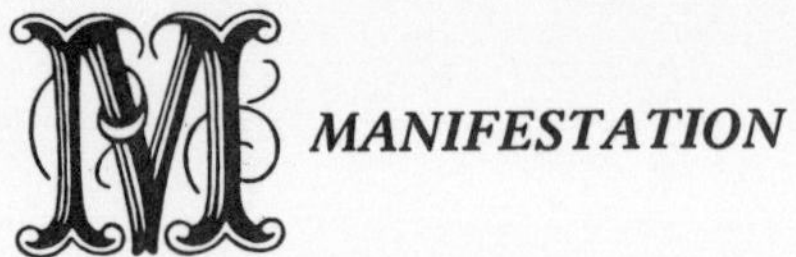 MANIFESTATION

> God's revelation
>   is an Avatar.
> An Avatar's manifestation
>   is God.

 NOTHING

> An Avatar's constant realisation is
>   that there is nothing
>   too great to achieve,
> and that nothing
>   is too small to receive.

 OPEN

> To please an Avatar
>   unconditionally and constantly
>   is to enter
>   into the open Heart
>   and Arms of God.

[46

PRACTICE

*An Avatar
  is God's daily practice
    of Infinite Compassion.*

QUESTION

*God's question an Avatar brings.
  Man's answer an Avatar takes.
God's question: Where is Life?
Man's answer: Life is where Love is.
  Life is God embodied.
    Love is God revealed.*

ROAD

*To have an Avatar-Guru
  is to run on the shortest road
    to God.*

 SALVATION

An Avatar
    is God's constant attention,
        heaven's brightest illumination
        and earth's sure salvation.

 TOUCH

Touch an Avatar devotedly,
    feel God unmistakably.

 UNION

The real Friend in an Avatar
    not only shows us God's Face,
our true union with God,
    and His Abode in us,
        but also makes us feel
that we can rightfully claim God
    as our very own.

VOICE

An Avatar
is the divinely illumined Choice
and supremely manifested
Voice of God.

WILL

God wills.
An Avatar executes.
Man either accepts or rejects.
When he accepts,
he becomes the light of life.
When he rejects,
he becomes the night of death.

X-RAY

The Supreme gives to the Avatars
his own X-Ray
to use at their sweet will
to see the malady of the millenia.
The Supreme has also given the Avatars
the power to cure the incurable malady
of the crying past,
screaming present
and weeping future.

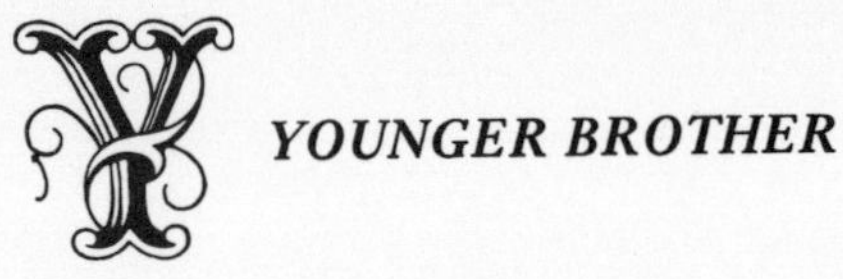 YOUNGER BROTHER

An Avatar's acceptance of a disciple
is the clear indication
of his eternal residence
in the heart
of his younger brother.

 ZOO

When an Avatar visits a zoo,
he amusingly enjoys
his own evolving past.
When he visits his Consciousness-Height,
he unceasingly admires
his own beginningless Past:
the Supreme of Light
and Delight Supreme.

THE DICTIONARY OF THE SUPREME

ASK

A surrendered seeker
gets everything from the Supreme
for the asking.
An unconditionally surrendered seeker
knows that the Supreme
has made him and calls him
His very own.

BUY

If you want to buy the perfect Perfection
of the Supreme from the Supreme,
then you have to sell
your imperfection-mountain and
ignorance-sea
free of charge to the Supreme.

CURIOUS

Man is curious to know
what the Supreme looks like.
The Supreme is eager to see
the cheerful arrival of man
at His Heart's Palace.

 *DIFFICULTY*

Man's difficulty is
  that he does not know
    when to start meditating.
The Supreme's difficulty is
  that He does not know
    when to stop bestowing
His unconditional Compassion on man.

 *ETERNITY*

Eternity: this is
  what man precisely needs.
Now: this is
  what the Supreme always wants.

 *FOOL*

Before God-realisation
  man was a fool
    and he behaved like a fool.
After his God-realisation
  man has become a pool
    and he serves as a pool.

 GATE

He who stands
at the Gate of the Supreme
knows that at long last
the reign of his fate has ended.
His life now has become
the rare choice of the Supreme.

 HISTORY

Man's eternal Aspiration
is the perfect History
of the Supreme.

 *IMPOSSIBILITY*

My constant choice
of the Supreme
commands
impossibility's surrendered life.

JOKE

Do you want
*   to cut jokes with the Supreme?*
Then devour Him
*   with your purified love,*
*   illumined devotion*
and fulfilled surrender.

KING

"Oh Supreme,
*   You are*
*   my aspiring life's only King."*
"True, My child,
*   I am also your surrendered heart's*
*   best and most unconditional slave."*

LIGHT

The Light of the Supreme
*   is His Life's Soul,*
*   His Soul's Goal,*
and His Goal's Role.

 MIND

The human mind
and the Will of the Supreme
are perfect strangers
to each other.

 NO

To value
the Compassion of the Supreme
is to say unmistakably
and categorically
"No"
to the proud life of ignorance.

 OBEDIENCE

A seeker's outer obedience
is his love for the Supreme.
A seeker's inner obedience
is the Supreme's Love for him.

PRAY

We pray to the Supreme
for illumining faith in Him.
The Supreme prays to us
for soaring confidence
in ourselves.

QUEEN

As the transcendental King,
the Supreme blesses
His infinite children.
As the transcendental Queen,
the Supreme embraces
Her infinite children.

REAL

To see the Supreme
face to face
is to own the breath and life
of the Real within us.

 SERVICE

*Man's fleeting service
    the Supreme unreservedly admires.
The Supreme's unending Service
    man constantly ignores.*

 TEMPTATION

*The desiring man
    and God the Temptation
        live together.
The aspiring man
    and God the Illumination
        fly together.*

 USE

*We use constantly
    the highest Compassion of the Supreme
        for our human satisfaction.
Poor Supreme will be able to use
    our heart's purest purity,
        if ever we have an iota of it,
for His divine Satisfaction.*

 *VOYAGE*

Man's love for the Supreme
must needs be a ceaseless voyage
to the shores
of Immortality's Infinity.

 *WHEN*

When I love the Supreme
as a human being,
He instructs and illumines me
as a Divine Being.

 *X-RAY*

The name
of the Supreme's X-Ray
is Compassion-Light.

 **YESTERDAY**

Yesterday
my Supreme touched my feet
and begged me to come out of
ignorance-night.
Today
my Supreme blesses
my fully awakened life.
Tomorrow
my Supreme will embrace
my totally surrendered life.

 **ZOO**

Except for the Supreme and His Light,
we are all chattering monkeys,
braying donkeys
and roaring lions
in the cosmic zoo.